*You are the most beautiful person
I know —
not just outside, but inside, too…
it means a lot to me
that you are my sister,
and I will love you forever.
A sister like you
is the greatest gift in the world.*

— *Kristy Jorgensen*

A Sister Is Forever

Is Forever

A Blue Mountain Arts® Collection
for One of the Most Beautiful
People You'll Ever Know

Edited by Gary Morris

Blue Mountain Press ™

SPS Studios, Inc., Boulder, Colorado

ISBN: 0-88396-642-5

ACKNOWLEDGMENTS appear on page 64.

Certain trademarks are used under license.

Manufactured in China.
Second Printing: 2002

 This book is printed on recycled paper.

*This book is printed on fine quality, laid embossed, 80 lb. paper. This paper has
been specially produced to be acid free (neutral pH) and contains no groundwood
or unbleached pulp. It conforms with all the requirements of the American
National Standards Institute, Inc., so as to ensure that this book will last and be
enjoyed by future generations.*

SPS Studios, Inc.
P.O. Box 4549, Boulder, Colorado 80306

Contents

You Are a Very Special Sister

I want you to know how amazing you are.
I want you to know how much you're
treasured and celebrated and quietly thanked.

I want you to feel really good... about who you are.
About all the great things you do!
I want you to appreciate your uniqueness.
Acknowledge your talents and abilities.
Realize what a beautiful soul you have.
Understand the wonder within.

You make so much sun shine through, and you
inspire so much joy in the lives of everyone who
is lucky enough to know you.

You are a very special person, giving so many
people a reason to smile. You deserve to receive
the best in return, and one of my heart's favorite
hopes is that the happiness you give away will
come back to warm you
    each and every day of your life.

— *Sydney Nealson*

A Sister's Love
Is Something to Cherish

A sister's love
is a love that fills the heart
with the sounds of laughter
echoing through time —
a sentimental soul to share your journey
and all the dreams between
the dark and the bright.
A sister's heart
is a place of warmth and caring,
written on the pages of your life —
a hand to lift your chin up
when you're down,
someone to hold on to
who is moved with sympathy.
A sister's power
is sunlight for your shadows
and memories growing stronger
through the winds of yesterday —
the eyes that see within your very being
all the good things you are yet to be.
A sister is a thousand memories
ringing their bells across your destiny —
all the happy sounds
of grace, love, and laughter.
A sister is someone
you'll always be so very grateful for.

— Linda E. Knight

No One Could Ever Take Your Place in My Life

There is no one I tell intimate details to
like I do you.
There's no one else I can count on
to always care.
There's no one who finds
the same things humorous
or who can lighten any situation.
There isn't another soul who understands me
and loves me anyway.
You are the one person I can always turn to,
whether it is to share heartache or joy.
You rejoice in my successes and applaud
my efforts.
You know just what to say, even in my
darkest moments.
You believe in me and encourage me
with your praise,
and you accept my faults and my hang-ups
unconditionally.
You may not be perfect in other people's eyes,
but you are perfect for me,
and there isn't a person in the world
who could ever take your place.

— *Barbara Cage*

The True Spirit of Sisters

*Sisters can be sweet sometimes
and not so sweet other times.
They can be silly and fun
or serious and demanding.
They can be happy and easygoing
or a bit grumpy and hardheaded.
But whatever words you use
to describe sisters,
you can never really capture
their true spirit, because…
A sister's true spirit
is found in her sensitive
and caring feelings that
are there when you need them.
That's just the way sisters are.*

*I hope the next time
you stop and think of me,
you'll remember how much
    I care about you
and know that we'll always be close;
we'll always have each other.*

— Dena Dilaconi

Thank You for Being My Sister and My Best Friend

*W*hen I reflect on all the fun we've shared over the years, I feel privileged being able to say that my sister is also my best friend. But life is more than laughter and the memories it makes. It's about family and caring and being there for each other no matter what.

If there's one thing I trust in this world, it's us. I know that wherever life takes me, you'll always be a central part of it. That reassurance comforts me and carries me over the shaky spots, magnifies the happy times, and makes my world a better one.

You've listened to me when I've needed to toss thoughts around. You've offered advice on request and somehow knew when I needed to hear the truth. You've given me space when you sensed silence was needed. And most of all, you've always been here for me through all the seasons of life. Forgiveness and unconditional love seem to be just a natural part of who you are.

I am so grateful for the fun in our friendship and the serious side that continues to love and support me without condition. No matter what is going on, your love insulates my world.

I can't believe how lucky I was to get a sister and best friend all in the same person! That makes me one of the luckiest people in the world.

— *Kathryn Leibovich*

I Wish You Life's Best

I wish that the sun will always
    shine for you,
and that your world
    will always be bright
        and warm and beautiful.
I wish the wonder of
    life's sweetest moments for you,
with hours full of happiness
    and days when everything
        goes the best it can.
I wish a million great beginnings
    for you,
with a perfect parade of
    all your dreams come true
and happy endings always.
I wish with all my heart
    for your greatest happiness.
I wish you nothing but the brilliant
    and vibrant colors of the rainbow
and life's brightest days...
because the sun should always
    shine for you.

— *Barbara J. Hall*

There's No One like a Sister

A sister is a part of your life
that you can never separate from.
Whether she's older or younger,
through all your formative years,
she shared your pain and sorrow,
your happiness and joy —
even when you were not aware
that she was there.
A sister protects you from all harm
and is always near when you need her.
She's a friend who listens forever
when others turn away.
She has the broadest shoulders
for you to lean on,
and never complains that you
cause too much trouble.

She asks for little in return —
just a portion of your time,
a few precious moments
to exchange secrets
as only sisters can do.
She brings sunshine where
there are clouds;
she is like a breath of spring
through the storms of winter,
a guiding star in the darkness of night.
She smiles at you when others frown
and welcomes you with open arms.
She accepts you for who you are
and doesn't expect you to be
anyone else.
She thinks that you're the best,
and makes you feel so important
that you start to believe it yourself.
There's no one like a sister...
and there's no sister like you!

— Geri Danks

Thanks to You, I Have So Many "Good Old Days" to Remember

We all have those "good old days"
tucked away in our hearts:
memories that make us smile,
journey with us as we move
    through time,
and give us special glimpses
    into yesterday.

We all have that place where
    we keep our best thoughts.
In that place, we can always be
    where laughter was in plenty,
and we can relive the happiest
    times of all,
        over and over again.

We all have our special memories —
those bright additions to each day.
I just wanted to let you know
    that mine are there...
because of you.

— Barbara J. Hall

Sister, You Have a Special Place in My Heart

There is never a time in my life
when I'm not with you in some way.
There are moments when you
come to mind more strongly,
sometimes in a special way,
but you are with me always.
Sometimes you are with me
in the warm memory
of some laughter we've shared.
I admire your personality,
your character, and
the qualities you possess.
You are a capable
and determined person.

There is an understanding
we have developed,
a relationship that shows we care,
and a oneness that has grown
out of respect, patience, and love.
If I could give you the happiness
and success that you deserve,
it would last forever.
I wish you all that you desire
and all that is beautiful.
You will forever be a part
of me and my life,
because you have a place in my heart.

— *Victor Barbella*

When Sisters Become Friends...

As family, sisters share
a very secure closeness.
But when friendship emerges
* from their closeness,*
something even more special happens...
A strong bond develops
that brings them even closer
* to each other.*
The bond is so powerful that
* it not only brings them added joy;*
it also comforts and befriends
* each sister with loyalty,*
compassion, and understanding
that cannot be measured.
Regardless of differences,
* miles between them,*
or anything that can separate them,
sisters who become friends are
always a part of each other.
They are the answer to each other's
* spoken and unspoken needs*
and always a gift of love
* to each other's heart.*

— Susan Hickman Sater

You're My Definition
of a Great Sister!

A great sister is someone
who knows how to share
her clothes and her books with me
and who allows me to join in
with her friends
and have fun together.

A great sister is someone
who is willing to talk late at night
about feelings,
and then not gossip about them
    with everyone the next day.
She understands what it means
to need someone
who is sincere and trustworthy.

This is what being a great sister
is all about.
In case you didn't know it,
I think that you're one of
the best sisters
anyone could ever have.
You do so many nice things for me,
and you care about my happiness.

So today, even though
a thousand other things
are happening in our lives,
I wanted to let you know
that I think you're a great sister.
I'm really glad for
the close relationship that we have.

— *Dena Dilaconi*

You Light Up the World

On the day you came into this world,
a beautiful star dropped from the sky
and landed in your heart.
You carry this wondrous light
within your soul,
and as you grow older
it begins to shine brighter,
making the world a happier place.
I think you are amazing,
truly unique in your kindness
and loving heart.
With each passing day,
I realize how truly blessed I am
to have you in my life.
You touch the hearts of those
around you,
sharing the incredible gift of you
and making me so proud
to be your sister.
I can only hope that one day
I can shine as brightly
as you do today.
May each day of your life
be just as wonderful as you are.

— Deana Marino

The Nine Secrets
of Our Sisterhood

1. We stay close. No matter how busy we are, we make time for keeping in touch. As sisters, we're never more than a heartbeat apart.

2. We spread happiness. When we have news to tell, we focus on the upbeat. We share jokes and laughter. In sad times, we fill one another with hope.

3. Our bond is one of respect. We value our differences, share our talents, and nurture one another's potential.

4. When it comes to each other's activities, we express interest. We are passionately interested in each other's life. That's what more-than-close friends are for.

5. We give each other support. We are the shelter in each other's storms. We lift each other's spirits and cheer one another on.

6. We are tops when it comes to trust. I can trust you with my secrets, and you can truly believe that I will keep yours under lock and key. We are loyal in sisterly love and devoted in our friendship.

7. We treasure our family memories. We are proud of where we came from, and we honor those who are our real-life family heroes.

8. We give each other personal attention. We listen with our hearts and help each other meet needs. We share the promise that someone will always be there to care about us.

9. We promote each other's success. We put any envy aside to promote one another. We are each other's highest achievement seekers.

These are the nine secrets of our sisterhood — but it's <u>no</u> secret that our sisterhood is at the top of our list of things to be thankful for.

— Jacqueline Schiff

As a Sister and a Woman, You're a Shining Example

The same qualities that
make you a terrific sister
also make you a wonderful woman...

You have a loving heart;
there are no limits to
your kindness, generosity,
and willingness to help.
If you have a fault,
it's that you always
put the needs of others
ahead of your own.

You are a woman of
many accomplishments,
but no matter how busy
you are, you never
lose sight of your priorities.
Your family always comes first.

You have been there for me
more times than I can count,
and I don't know what
I'd do without you.

— Patricia A. Teckelt

Sister, I Hope You Remember All the Things That Dreams Are Made Of

Remember: if you can dream it,
you can probably make it come true.
Build wonderful bridges to get
where you're going.
Appreciate all the special qualities
within you.

Don't let worries get in the way of
recognizing how great things can be.
Don't look back; always move ahead.
Live to the fullest; make each day count.
Don't let the important things go unsaid.

Don't just have minutes in the day; have
moments in time. Balance out any bad
with the good you can provide. Know
that you are capable of amazing results.
Surprise yourself by discovering new
strength inside.

Add a meaningful page to the diary of each day. Do things no one else would even <u>dream</u> of. There is no greater gift than the kind of inner beauty you possess. Do the things you do… with love.

Walk along the pathways that enrich your happiness. Taking care of the "little things" is a big necessity. Don't be afraid of testing your courage. Life is short, but it's long enough to have excitement <u>and</u> serenity.

Do the things that brighten your life and help you on your way. Don't just dream of a successful journey; <u>begin</u> <u>it</u>. Know how much I care about you.

And remember…
    one of life's nicest presents
     is your presence in it.

— *Collin McCarty*

Never Forget This,
My Sister...

The sun keeps shining
even when the clouds roll in.
Though they may block the view
for a short time,
together we can chase them away
and find happy days again.

I know things aren't always easy,
but I want you to remember
that I'll be behind you
every step of the way,
reminding you how wonderful you are
and how bright the days ahead will be.

Just know that life does not give us
more than we can handle.
But when it seems that way,
I'll be right beside you,
ready to ease your heart
and lighten your load.
Together we will clear the skies
to brighter days.

— Vincent Arcoleo

As Sisters,
We Share So Much

We *share a variety of memories*
that bond us to our childhood,
and a wealth of joys
that I will cherish forever.
Back then, there was a friendship
between us that brought comfort
and an affinity within our hearts
that still prevails.
When we were young,
we had everything in each other...
We shared warm smiles,
we loved and supported each other
throughout the triumph and the pain,
and we relied on each other
to ease our sorrows and
to share our tears.
We laid the framework for
a precious bond that unites our hearts.

As sisters,
we spent some of the most
invaluable moments of our lives
by each other's side.
I accomplished some of my
brightest dreams
because of your confidence in me.
We share memories of our past
and dreams of our future.
I want you to know
that within my heart,
I know what truly means the most to me...
the love and compassion of a sister
as wonderful as you.

— Shannon M. Lester

I Wish Everyone Could Have
a Sister like You

When things don't go as planned,
you're the first one there beside me —
someone to count on,
someone who cares.
When the world has lost its luster,
you never lose your faith in me —
and somehow, through the clouds,
I find my wings.
You're the door that's always open,
arms spread wide,
and deep conversations long into the night.
You're a shelter for my soul,
the key to my diary,
and a journal of memories
through time and years.
You're my light in the darkness,
laughter in the night,
and all the things that keep me going
on life's unwinding road.
You're a special kind of person,
a unique and caring friend,
and a wonderful woman.
I know I'm really lucky,
and I wish everyone could have
a sister like you.

— Linda E. Knight

Sisters...
Always and Forever

An age difference kept us from being very close when we were children, but as time went by and we grew, that gap became smaller and smaller.

We went separate ways and began our lives; all the while, we were growing and becoming the women we are today. Distance could never change the love in our hearts, and time would only bring a deeper understanding of each other and the lives we had built for ourselves.

You were always there for me, and I hope I have done the same for you. You have always been more than a sister to me; you have been my friend.

I would never find a truer friend if I were to search until my dying day. Not many sisters can have what we have. We can share our triumphs and defeats, our laughter and tears, and — always — our dreams.

You have helped in many ways to make me the woman I am today. You have been someone I can look up to, someone who has set out to conquer the world and has accomplished so many great things — which always makes me proud to say that you are my sister.

Always remember, dear one, that no matter where you are or what you do, I will always be there for you.

All you have to do is call, and I will be there.

— Deanna Casey

A Sister like You
Is the Best Present of All

You and I have been given a gift...
that began by being invaluable
and that has grown even more
precious through the years.
It is the lovely gift... of being sisters.

It is a gift that is exquisite in
all the ways that matter — one
that spends its days understanding,
supporting, making the best kind
of memories there are, and simply
helping one another rise above.

We share the gift of being sisters...
and in every season of our lives,
we'll be blessed with the strongest
friendship and bound by the deepest love.

— Marin McKay

No One Knows Me
Better than You, Sister

*Our hearts are intertwined in a
history of shared memories. We
lived the same childhood, broke many
of the same rules, and learned lessons
from each other and from life.
Because of this, you understand not
only where I've come from, but who
I really am.
We each have chosen our own path in
life. Yet our paths inevitably converge
again and again as time goes by, for
we never lose sight of their origin.*

Over the years, we've talked and laughed,
listened and cried, supported and
understood in ways no one else could.
Even when we don't see eye to eye, I
know you only want the best for me —
just as I do for you.
No matter what else happens in my life —
no matter how many times I change
direction or make mistakes — I know
you will always be there for me.
Your love is very special. It centers me
and takes me back. It challenges me
and leads me forward. I'm so glad that
we will always be sisters and friends.

— Pamela Koehlinger

I Appreciate
Everything We Share

*While we often approach life differently,
we can discuss anything, sharing our thoughts
openly. You remember our good old days, so we
can start from the same page. We were taught
the same values and saw many of the same
situations, so I can really appreciate your
support and insight. You don't pull any punches
and often warn me or make me think through
my actions.*

*Though we may disagree sometimes or have
trouble in our lives, our bond will always be
there. We both know that, though our lives
may be busy, if either of us needed each other,
we would drop everything and come. You're
my sister, and I love you with all my heart.*

— *Sandra Fubini*

Sisters Are Always There for Each Other

Sisters help each other; they give counsel to one another; they understand. Sisters don't desert you when you're discouraged. They offer you support. They volunteer. They don't wait or turn the other way. They take risks for each other. They go out of their way for you, and their gift in return is just knowing that they have helped you. And they would do the same thing again for no reason other than because they want to help.

Sisters pick each other up when they are down. They help each other find their way when they're lost. They're sensitive to one another's insecurities. They give you their umbrella to shield you from the rain when they know you're going through a storm. They thank you when you help to answer their prayer, and they always remember what you did for them.

*They're strong when you're weak and wobbly,
and when they're weak, you're strong for
them. Sisters hang in there with you until
they see that you're standing straight with
both feet on the ground.*

*Sisters listen and they support and they share.
They don't talk about you behind your back.
They don't judge you. They advise. They help.
They care. They treat you like they want you
to treat them. Their lives blend together in
harmony. They turn the ups and downs of life
into rhythms with a little more rhyme and a
little more reason and understanding. They
lighten your load when you're too tired to go
on. They remind you that you're strong and
you can get through whatever it is you're
going through and that they will be there
with you through it all.*

— *Donna Fargo*

I know that I can depend on you in any emergency or for any favor. I know you understand my moods, my needs, my heart. I can always count on you to laugh with me (that is one of my favorite things about us), and I probably laugh with you more than with anyone else in the world.

I can always count on you to listen and to be honest when you disagree, yet I'm secure in the knowledge that no disagreement or problem will ever be big enough to come between us.

You are one of the most important people in my life. There are sisters and there are friends, but it doesn't get any better than having the love and memories I share with my sister combined with the humor, respect, and fun we share as friends.

— Barbara Cage

To the Angel in My Life...
My Sister

Sometimes you are lucky enough
to experience (and recognize)
a glimpse of the light that is
Knowledge and Love
in their purest forms,
and an unseen hand pauses
to touch your brow
and smooth away uncertainty
    and fear.
Some of us call this hand
    an angel...

When an angel touches you,
you are left with
a feeling of peace,
a message of hope,
and a brighter life.

I want to thank you
for being one of the angels
who has alighted upon my spirit
and blessed my life.

— Gina Breitkreutz

Sisters Have a Special Way
of Growing Closer Through the Years

*Girls will be girls
and friends will be friends,
but when you think of
sisters being sisters,
you know exactly how close
the feelings can be.
Sisters have a special way
of growing closer as the years go by,
and the feelings they have shared
are always a very important part
of their lives.*

*And though sisters may disagree at times,
they ultimately accept each other
for the way they are,
and they know that
what really matters is the love
they feel for one another.*

— Deanna Beisser

You Are
the Most Beautiful Person I Know

You are the most beautiful person
I know —
not just outside, but inside, too.
You have a wonderful sense of humor,
a loyalty that not many people have,
and a gift of love you give to others.

We may not be perfect —
we have our share of arguments,
our times of laughter,
and our share of troubles.
Yet we can always trust
each other with anything.

When you just have to share something,
good or bad,
I will listen.
You are the world to me.
Words can't express my appreciation,
but it means a lot to me
that you are my sister,
and I will love you forever.
A sister like you
is the greatest gift in the world.

— Kristy Jorgensen

I've Been Blessed
with a Beautiful Sister!

Maybe someday I'll be able to find all the right words to tell you how much you mean to me. In the meantime, I just hope you know, deep within your heart, that having you as my sister is a gift I thank my lucky stars for.

You're such a precious part of my life. Our family ties and our deep, lasting friendship comprise a special love that always sees me through. If I hadn't been blessed with such a beautiful sister, I would have spent a lifetime... wishing for someone just like you.

— Laurel Atherton

Sister, May You Always Have...

Cheer to greet you each morning, so each new day will help you believe that you are one step closer to your dreams.

Peace in your inner being so you can breathe easy and enjoy every moment of your life.

Faith to encourage and inspire you; to comfort you and heal your hurts; to commune with and be one with; to help you get in touch with your true self.

Laughter to bring you happiness and fun and keep your joy alive; to remind you that life is too short to spend it crying.

Beauty to fill your eyes with the simple
gifts that nature brings.

Confidence to do all the things that your
true self desires; to conquer your fears
and be free to reach your goals.

Friendships that are lasting and true
with people who respect your values
and are full of sharing and caring.

Memories that are warm and comforting
and that you can reflect on and smile
about: memories of our times together —
loving memories that last a long while.

— Jacqueline Schiff

A Sister Is Forever

My sister...
you're the one who's shared so much with me
Our time together goes way back before we ever
thought about a time apart —
a time when we would go our separate ways
a time when we'd no longer have that instant
access into each other's thoughts and feelings
I miss those days we used to spend together —
those caring, sharing times that kept us close
that seemed so permanently etched
into our lives
we couldn't imagine a moment apart
But now we are apart
and now my heart's determined
to find another way to share some time with you
to make sure you know
that no matter how many miles
come between you and me
nothing else ever will
because we're sisters
and a sister is forever

My sister...
you're the one who is always in my heart

— Barbara J. Hall

ACKNOWLEDGMENTS

The following is a partial list of authors whom the publisher especially wishes to thank for permission to reprint their works.

Linda E. Knight for "A Sister's Love Is Something to Cherish" and "I Wish Everyone Could Have a Sister like You." Copyright © 2002 by Linda E. Knight. All rights reserved.

Barbara Cage for "No One Could Ever Take Your Place in My Life." Copyright © 2002 by Barbara Cage. All rights reserved.

Kathryn Leibovich for "Thank You for Being My Sister...." Copyright © 2002 by Kathryn Leibovich. All rights reserved.

Barbara J. Hall for "Thanks to You, I Have So Many..." and "A Sister Is Forever." Copyright © 2002 by Barbara J. Hall. All rights reserved.

Jacqueline Schiff for "The Nine Secrets of Our Sisterhood." Copyright © 2002 by Jacqueline Schiff. All rights reserved.

Patricia A. Teckelt for "As a Sister and a Woman...." Copyright © 2002 by Patricia A. Teckelt. All rights reserved.

Shannon M. Lester for "As Sisters, We Share So Much." Copyright © 2002 by Shannon M. Lester. All rights reserved.

Deanna Casey for "Sisters... Always and Forever." Copyright © 2002 by Deanna Casey. All rights reserved.

PrimaDonna Entertainment Corp. for "Sisters Are Always There for Each Other" by Donna Fargo. Copyright © 1999, 2002 by PrimaDonna Entertainment Corp. All rights reserved.

A careful effort has been made to trace the ownership of poems used in this anthology in order to obtain permission to reprint copyrighted materials and give proper credit to the copyright owners. If any error or omission has occurred, it is completely inadvertent, and we would like to make corrections in future editions provided that written notification is made to the publisher:

SPS STUDIOS, INC., P.O. Box 4549, Boulder, Colorado 80306.